TREATS

just great recipes

GENERAL INFORMATION

The level of difficulty of the recipes in this book
is expressed as a number from 1 (simple) to 3 (difficult).

TREATS
just great recipes

penne fusilli
&co.

McRae Books

Types of Short Pasta

The most common short pasta types—penne, fusilli, cavatappi, conchiglie, farfalle, eliche, maccheroni, rigatoni, and ruote—are just a few among the dozens of shapes to be found in Italy. There are also regional varieties (garganelli, malloreddus) and flavored and colored versions (mainly for the tourists), as well as a host of small pasta types usually used in soups. Despite their differences in shape, almost all the most popular short pasta types are made commercially using hard durum wheat flour and water.

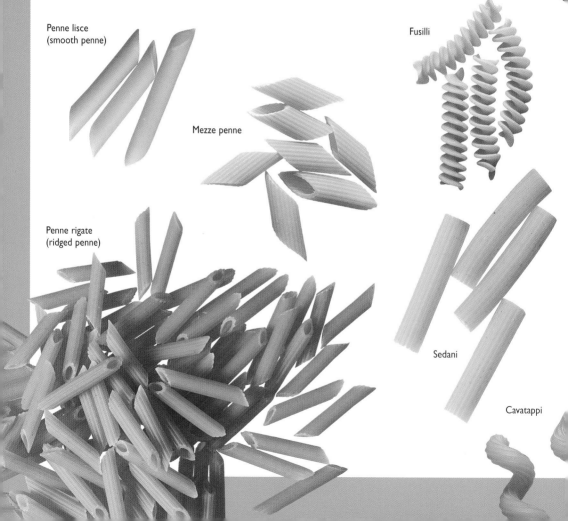

Penne nero
(penne with
squid's ink)

Penne lisce
(smooth penne)

Fusilli

Mezze penne

Penne rigate
(ridged penne)

Sedani

Cavatappi

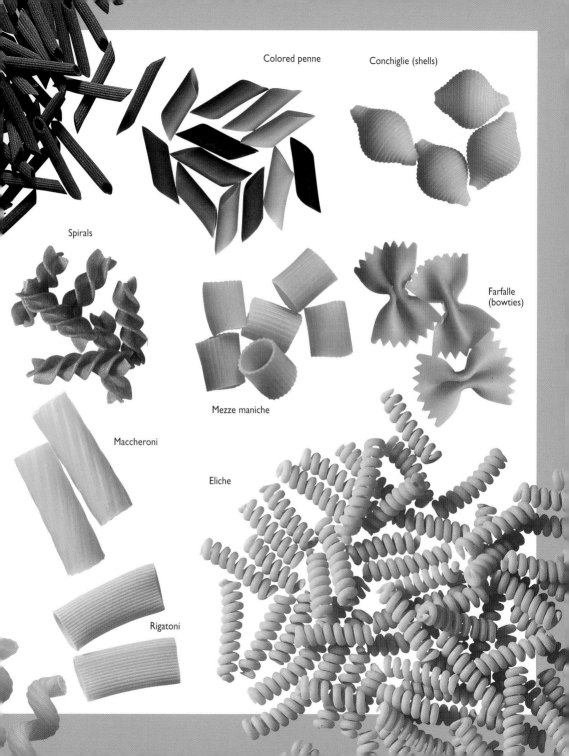

Colored penne

Conchiglie (shells)

Spirals

Farfalle
(bowties)

Mezze maniche

Maccheroni

Eliche

Rigatoni

SERVES 4–6

PREPARATION 10 min

COOKING 15 min

DIFFICULTY level 1

Garganelli
with speck

Bring a large pot of salted water to a boil over high heat. • Sauté the onion in 2 tablespoons of butter in a large frying pan over medium heat until softened, about 5 minutes. • In a separate frying pan, sauté the speck in the remaining 2 tablespoons of butter over medium heat until crisp, 2–3 minutes (bacon will take a little longer). • Add the speck to the onion. • Cook the pasta in the boiling water until very al dente (1–2 minutes less than the instructions on the package). • Drain, reserving 5 tablespoons of the cooking water. Add the pasta and cooking water to the pan with the sauce and toss until the pasta is cooked. • Serve hot.

2 onions, finely chopped
¼ cup (60 g) butter
1 cup (120 g) speck or smoked bacon, cut into thin strips
1 lb (500 g) g dried garganelli, penne, or other short pasta shape

Rigatoni
with onion sauce

Bring a large pot of salted water to a boil over high heat. • Melt the butter in a medium saucepan over low heat. • Add the onion and sweat until softened and pale golden brown, about 20 minutes. • Increase the heat to medium, pour in the wine, and cook until it evaporates, about 5 minutes. • Cook the pasta in the boiling water until al dente. • Drain and add to the pan with the sauce. Season with salt and pepper. Sprinkle with Pecorino and toss gently. • Serve hot.

⅔ cup (150 g) butter or diced pork lard

2 large white onions, finely chopped

¼ cup (60 ml) dry white wine

1 lb (500 g) rigatoni or other short pasta shape

Salt and freshly ground black pepper

4–6 tablespoons freshly grated Pecorino or Parmesan cheese

SERVES 4–6
PREPARATION 15 min
COOKING 15 min
DIFFICULTY level 1

Penne
with walnut sauce

Bring a large pot of salted water to a boil over high heat. • Melt the butter in a frying pan over medium heat. Add the garlic and sauté until softened, 2–3 minutes. • Add the walnuts and sauté for 2 minutes. • Stir in the cream. Simmer over low heat until the sauce thickens, about 12 minutes. Season with salt and white pepper. • Meanwhile, cook the pasta in the boiling water until al dente. Drain well and add to the pan with the walnut sauce. • Toss gently for 30 seconds. Sprinkle with the marjoram and serve hot.

5 tablespoons butter
2 cloves garlic, finely chopped
40 walnuts, coarsely chopped
1 cup (250 ml) heavy (double) cream
Salt and freshly ground white pepper
1 lb (500 g) penne rigate
2 tablespoons finely chopped marjoram

SERVES 4–6

PREPARATION 20 min + 30 min to chill

COOKING 15 min

DIFFICULTY level 1

Farfalle Salad
with cherry tomatoes and olives

Cook the pasta in a large pot of salted boiling water until al dente. • Drain and cool under cold running water. Drain thoroughly and dry on a clean cloth. Transfer to a large salad bowl. Add 2 tablespoons of the oil and toss well. • Add the tomatoes, capers, mozzarella, olives, and basil. Mix well. • Heat the remaining oil in a small frying pan over medium heat. Add the garlic and sauté until pale golden brown, 3–4 minutes. • Add the anchovies and sauté, crushing with a fork, until dissolved, 3–4 minutes. • Drizzle this mixture over the salad and toss well. Chill for 30 minutes before serving.

1 lb (500 g) farfalle

1/4 cup (60 ml) extra-virgin olive oil

20 cherry tomatoes, halved

1 tablespoon capers preserved in salt, rinsed

8 oz (250 g) fresh mozzarella, drained and cut into small cubes

Generous 1/2 cup (60 g) black olives, pitted

1 tablespoon finely chopped basil

2 cloves garlic, finely chopped

4 anchovy fillets preserved in oil, drained

Farfalle
with peas and scallions

Bring a large pot of salted water to a boil over high heat. • Heat the oil in a large frying pan over medium heat. Add the pancetta and scallions. Sauté until the onions are tender and the pancetta is crisp and lightly browned, about 5 minutes. • Add the flour and mix well. Pour in the stock and wine and mix well. Bring to a boil. • Add the peas and cook until the peas are tender and the sauce has thickened. Season with salt and pepper. Mix well and remove from the heat. • Meanwhile, cook the pasta in the boiling water until al dente. • Drain well and add to the pan with the sauce. Sprinkle with parsley and toss over high heat for 1 minute. • Serve hot.

1/4 cup (60 ml) extra-virgin olive oil
5 oz (150 g) pancetta or bacon, chopped
8 scallions (spring onions), thinly sliced
2 tablespoons all-purpose (plain) flour
1 cup (250 ml) vegetable stock (homemade or bouillon cube)
1/2 cup (125 ml) dry white wine
1 1/2 cups (400 g) frozen peas
Salt and freshly ground black pepper
1 lb (500 g) farfalle
2 tablespoons finely chopped parsley

Penne
with gorgonzola and cream

Bring a large pot of salted water to a boil over high heat. • Heat the butter and Gorgonzola with the cream in a double boiler over barely simmering water until the cheese has melted. Season with salt, 5–7 minutes. • Meanwhile, cook the pasta in the boiling water until al dente. • Drain and add to the cheese mixture. Mix well so that the pasta is coated with the sauce. Sprinkle with Parmesan. • Serve hot.

¼ cup (60 g) butter

12 oz (350 g) Gorgonzola cheese, crumbled

⅔ cup (150 ml) heavy (double) cream

Salt

1 lb (500 g) penne

½ cup (60 g) freshly grated Parmesan

SERVES 4

PREPARATION 15 min

COOKING 20 min

DIFFICULTY level 1

Soup Pasta
with fava beans

Heat the oil and butter in a medium saucepan over medium heat. •
Add the pancetta and onion and sauté until the onion is softened,
about 5 minutes. • Stir in the fava beans and pour in the water. •
Bring to a boil and simmer gently until the fava beans are almost
tender, about 10 minutes. • Add the pasta, season with salt, and cook
until the pasta is just al dente. If, as you cook the pasta, there is not
enough liquid, add a little more water. • Season with pepper and
sprinkle with Pecorino. Serve hot.

2 tablespoons extra-virgin olive oil
2 tablespoons butter
1/2 cup (60 g) diced pancetta or bacon
1 onion, finely chopped
2 cups (300 g) frozen fava (broad) beans
3 cups (750 ml) cold water + more as needed
12 oz (350 g) dried soup pasta, such as ditali
Salt and freshly ground black pepper
1/2 cup (60 g) freshly grated Pecorino

Rigatoni
with pecorino and lemon

Bring a large pot of salted water to a boil over high heat. • Melt the butter in a medium frying pan over high heat. • Mix in the lemon juice, saffron, and Pecorino. Remove from the heat and set aside. • Cook the pasta in the boiling water until al dente. • Drain well and add to the sauce. Toss gently and serve hot.

$^1/_3$ cup (90 g) butter

Juice and finely grated zest of 2 lemons

$^1/_2$ teaspoon saffron threads, crumbled

2 cups (250 g) freshly grated Pecorino cheese

1 lb (500 g) rigatoni

SERVES 4–6

PREPARATION 15 min

COOKING 15 min

DIFFICULTY level 1

Garganelli
with creamy sausage sauce

Bring a large pot of salted water to a boil over high heat. • Heat 1 tablespoon of butter in a large frying pan over medium heat. Add the onion and sauté until softened, about 5 minutes. • Add the sausage and sauté over high heat until browned all over, about 3 minutes. • Pour in the cream and simmer over very low heat, about 10 minutes. • Season with nutmeg, salt, and pepper. • Meanwhile, cook the pasta in the boiling water until al dente. • Drain and add to the sauce. • Sprinkle with the Parmesan and parsley and toss gently. • Serve hot.

3 tablespoons butter
1 onion, finely chopped
1 lb (500 g) Italian pork sausage, crumbled
$3/4$ cup (180 ml) heavy (double) cream
$1/4$ teaspoon freshly grated nutmeg
Salt and freshly ground black pepper
1 lb (500 g) dried garganelli or penne
$1/2$ cup (60 g) freshly grated Parmesan
1 tablespoon finely chopped parsley

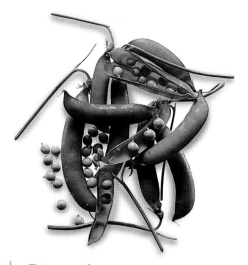

SERVES 4–6

PREPARATION 15 min

COOKING 20 min

DIFFICULTY level 1

Sedanini
with peas and sausage

Bring a large pot of salted water to a boil over high heat. • Heat the butter in a medium saucepan over medium heat. Add the onion and sauté until softened, about 5 minutes. • Stir in the tomato sauce and sausage. Pour in the cream and simmer over low heat for 15 minutes. • Sauté the garlic and sage in the oil in a medium saucepan over low heat until the garlic is pale gold, about 3 minutes. • Stir in the peas, sugar, and water. Simmer until the peas are tender, about 10 minutes. • Season with salt and pepper and add the parsley. • Meanwhile, cook the pasta in the boiling water until al dente. • Drain the pasta and add to the sauce together with the cream and sausage mixture. Toss well. • Sprinkle with the Parmesan and serve hot.

2 tablespoons butter
1 onion, finely chopped
2 tablespoons unseasoned tomato sauce, store-bought or homemade
1 lb (500 g) Italian sausage, crumbled
1/2 cup (125 ml) heavy (double) cream
1 clove garlic, finely chopped
1 small bunch fresh sage, finely chopped
2 tablespoons extra-virgin olive oil
2 cups (300 g) frozen peas
1/8 teaspoon sugar
1 cup (250 ml) hot water, + more as needed
Salt and freshly ground black pepper
2 tablespoons finely chopped parsley
1 lb (500 g) sedanini or penne
1/2 cup (60 g) freshly grated Parmesan

SERVES 4–6

PREPARATION 15 min

COOKING 20 min

DIFFICULTY level 1

Ruote
with pesto and cherry tomatoes

Bring a large pot of salted water to a boil over high heat. • Toast the pine nuts in a large frying pan over medium heat until lightly browned, about 3 minutes. Set aside. • Toast the almonds in a large frying pan over medium heat until lightly browned, about 3 minutes. • Purée the garlic and basil in a food processor until smooth. Add the almonds and Pecorino and blend until smooth. Season with salt and pepper. Gradually add the oil, blending continuously, until the pesto is thick and smooth. • Cook the pasta in the boiling water until al dente. Drain well, reserving 3 tablespoons of the cooking liquid. • Add the reserved cooking liquid to the pesto and mix well. Add the pesto, tomatoes and pine nuts to the pasta and toss well. Garnish with basil and serve hot.

1/4 cup (45 g) pine nuts
Generous 1/2 cup (90 g) blanched almonds
4 cloves garlic
1 bunch basil + extra leaves, to garnish
1/3 cup (50 g) freshly grated Pecorino
Salt and freshly ground black pepper
1/3 cup (90 ml) extra-virgin olive oil
1 lb (500 g) ruote or other short pasta
1 lb (500 g) cherry tomatoes, cut in half

SERVES 4–6

PREPARATION 15 min

COOKING 15 min

DIFFICULTY level 1

Fusilli
with ricotta and dried tomatoes

Bring a large pot of salted water to a boil over high heat. • Beat together the ricotta, mint, and parsley in a bowl with a fork to make a smooth cream. Season with salt and pepper. • Place the tomatoes in a bowl and add the garlic, capers, and oil. Mix well. • Chop the arugula and tomato mixture in a food processor to make a smooth paste. • Cook the pasta in the boiling water until al dente. • Drain well, reserving 3 tablespoons of the cooking liquid. • Transfer the pasta to a heated serving bowl. • Stir the reserved cooking liquid into the pesto. Add the ricotta and pesto to the pasta and toss well. • Garnish with arugula and serve hot.

1 lb (500 g) fresh ricotta, drained
1 tablespoon finely chopped mint
1 tablespoon finely chopped parsley
Salt and freshly ground black pepper
4 oz (125 g) sun-dried tomatoes, soaked in warm water for 15 minutes, drained, and chopped
1 clove garlic, finely chopped
1 tablespoon salt-cured capers, rinsed
1/3 cup (90 ml) extra-virgin olive oil
4 oz (125 g) arugula (rocket), chopped, + extra leaves, to garnish
1 lb (500 g) fusilli

SERVES 4–6

PREPARATION 30 min

COOKING 1 h 30 min

DIFFICULTY level 2

Penne
with crabmeat

Stock: Bring the water to a boil in a large saucepan with the onion, celery, tomato, stalks of parsley, garlic, and salt. Simmer for 15 minutes. • Add the crabs and simmer for 20 minutes. Drain, reserving the stock. • Cool the crabs to lukewarm, then remove the flesh from the shells, leaving the claws whole. • Sauce: Sauté the garlic, 1 tablespoon of parsley, the chile, and sage in the oil in a large saucepan until the garlic is pale gold, 2–3 minutes. • Stir in the tomatoes, the crab claws, salt, and pepper, and simmer for 15 minutes. • Add the crabmeat and pour in 2 cups (500 ml) of the stock. Simmer over low heat for 30 minutes. • Cook the pasta in a large pot of salted boiling water until al dente. Drain, transfer to the sauce and toss well. • Sprinkle with the parsley, dot with the remaining butter, letting it melt into the pasta, and serve hot.

Stock
3 quarts (3 liters) cold water
1 red onion, sliced
1 stalk celery, sliced
1 firm-ripe tomato
3–4 stalks parsley
1 clove garlic
1 teaspoon salt
2 lb (1 kg) large crabs, cleaned

Sauce
2 cloves garlic, chopped
2 tablespoons finely chopped parsley
1 dried chile pepper, finely chopped
1 bunch fresh sage, finely chopped
5 tablespoons extra-virgin olive oil
1½ lb (700 g) tomatoes, peeled, seeded, and coarsely chopped
Salt and freshly ground black pepper
1 lb (500 g) penne
1 tablespoon butter

SERVES 4–6

PREPARATION 15 min

COOKING 35 min

DIFFICULTY level 1

Penne

with tomato and mushrooms

Bring a large pot of salted water to a boil over high heat. • Heat the oil in a large frying pan over medium heat. Add the garlic and sauté until pale golden brown, 2–3 minutes. • Add the pancetta and sauté until crisp and brown, about 5 minutes. • Add the mushrooms and tomatoes and season with salt and pepper. Sauté until the mushrooms are tender and the sauce has reduced a little, about 20 minutes. • Stir in the cream and simmer for 2–3 minutes. • Meanwhile, cook the pasta in the boiling water until al dente. Drain well and add to the sauce. • Add two-thirds of the cheese and toss well. Sprinkle with the remaining cheese and serve hot.

1/4 cup (60 ml) extra-virgin olive oil
2 cloves garlic, lightly crushed but whole
4 oz (125 g) pancetta or bacon, chopped
14 oz (400 g) button mushrooms, sliced
Salt and freshly ground black pepper
1 green chile pepper, seeded and sliced
2 (14-oz/400 g) cans tomatoes, with juice
1/3 cup (90 ml) heavy (double) cream
1 lb (500 g) penne
1/2 cup (60 g) freshly grated Pecorino or Parmesan

Penne
with meat sauce

Heat the butter in a large frying pan over medium heat. Add the carrot, celery, and onion and sauté until softened, about 5 minutes. • Add the pork and beef and sauté until browned, 5–7 minutes. • Add the ham and cook for 1 minute. • Increase the heat to high, pour in the wine, and let it evaporate, about 5 minutes. • Stir in the tomatoes. Season with salt, pepper, and nutmeg. • Partially cover the pan and simmer over low heat for about 1 hour. • Cook the pasta in a large pot of salted boiling water until al dente. Drain well and add to the sauce. • Add the cheese and toss well. Serve hot.

1 carrot, finely chopped
2 stalks celery, finely chopped
1 medium onion, finely chopped
2 tablespoons butter
1 lb (500 g) ground (minced) pork
5 oz (150 g) ground (minced) beef
1 cup (125 g) diced ham
2/3 cup (150 ml) dry white wine
6 large tomatoes,
    peeled and coarsely chopped
Salt and freshly ground black pepper
1/4 teaspoon freshly ground nutmeg
1 lb (500 g) penne
1/2 cup (60 g) freshly grated Parmesan

SERVES 4–6

PREPARATION 5 min

COOKING 15 min

DIFFICULTY level 1

Macaroni
with egg and cheese

Cook the pasta in a large pot of salted boiling water until just al dente. Drain well. • Heat the oil in a large frying pan over medium heat. Add the pasta and sauté for 2 minutes. • Beat the eggs, Pecorino, and parsley in a medium bowl. Season with salt and pepper. • Pour the egg mixture into the frying pan with the pasta. Toss well until the egg is cooked through, 2–3 minutes. • Serve hot.

1 lb (500 g) macaroni or other short pasta shape
½ cup (125 ml) extra-virgin olive oil
4–6 large eggs
1 cup (125 g) freshly grated Parmesan
2 tablespoons finely chopped parsley
Salt and freshly ground black pepper

SERVES 4–6

PREPARATION 15 min

COOKING 35 min

DIFFICULTY level 1

Penne
with swordfish and salmon

Bring a large pot of salted water to a boil over high heat. • Heat the oil in a large frying pan over medium heat. Add the garlic and onion and sauté until softened, about 5 minutes. • Add the swordfish and salmon. Sauté for 3 minutes. • Add the wine and cook until it evaporates, about 4 minutes. • Remove the fish and set aside. • Add the tomatoes and simmer over medium-low heat for 15 minutes. • Return the fish to the pan. Add the parsley, season with salt, and simmer for 2–3 minutes. • Meanwhile, cook the pasta in the boiling water until al dente. • Drain well and add to the sauce. Toss gently over high heat for 1 minute. • Serve hot.

¼ cup (60 ml) extra-virgin olive oil
1 clove garlic, finely chopped
1 small onion, finely chopped
4 oz (125 g) swordfish,
    cut into bite-size chunks
4 oz (125 g) salmon,
    cut into bite-size chunks
⅓ cup (90 ml) dry white wine
1 lb (500 g) cherry tomatoes, halved
2 tablespoons finely chopped parsley
Salt
1 lb (500 g) penne

29

SERVES 6

PREPARATION 10 min

COOKING 15 min

DIFFICULTY level 1

Macaroni
with sweet cocoa sauce

Cook the pasta in a large pot of salted boiling water until al dente. • Drain and transfer to a large bowl. Stir in the butter. • Add the sugar, walnuts, cocoa, bread crumbs, cinnamon, and lemon zest and toss well. • Serve hot.

1 lb (500 g) macaroni or other short pasta shape
1/3 cup (90 g) butter
1/2 cup (100 g) sugar
3 cups (300 g) finely chopped walnuts
1/2 cup (75 g) unsweetened cocoa powder
1 cup (125 g) fine dry bread crumbs
1/2 teaspoon ground cinnamon
Finely grated zest of 1 large lemon

SERVES 4–6

PREPARATION 15 min

COOKING 30 min

DIFFICULTY level 1

Penne
with spicy tomato sauce

Bring a large pot of salted water to a boil over high heat. • Sauté the pancetta in the oil in a frying pan over medium heat until crisp, about 5 minutes. • Use a slotted spoon to transfer the pancetta to a heated plate. • In the same oil, sauté the chile pepper and garlic until the garlic is pale gold, 2–3 minutes. • Stir in the tomatoes and season with salt. Add the parsley and simmer until the tomatoes have broken down, 15–20 minutes. • Add the pancetta and cook for 3 minutes. • Meanwhile, cook the pasta in the boiling water until al dente. Drain and add to the sauce. Toss well. • Sprinkle with the Pecorino and serve hot.

5 oz (150 g) pancetta or bacon, cut into small strips

1/3 cup (90 ml) extra-virgin olive oil

2 fresh spicy red chile peppers

5 cloves garlic, finely chopped

2 lb (1 kg) tomatoes, peeled and coarsely chopped

Salt

1 tablespoon finely chopped parsley

1 lb (500 g) dried penne

1/2 cup (60 g) freshly grated Pecorino cheese

SERVES 4–6

PREPARATION 20 min

COOKING 30 min

DIFFICULTY level 2

Maccheroni
with bell peppers

Heat the broiler (grill) on a high setting. Place the bell peppers under the heat and grill, turning often, until the skins are blackened all over. • Wrap the bell peppers in a paper bag and let rest for 5 minutes. Unwrap and remove the skins and seeds. Rinse and dry well. Slice thinly. • Bring a large pot of salted water to a boil over high heat. • Sauté the bell peppers in 3 tablespoons of the oil in a frying pan over high heat for 2 minutes. Season with salt and remove from the heat. • Sauté the garlic in the remaining oil in a large frying pan over medium heat until pale gold, 2–3 minutes. • Stir in the tomatoes and cook over high heat for 5 minutes. • Season with salt and add the parsley. Remove from the heat. • Meanwhile, cook the pasta in the boiling water until al dente. • Drain well. Add the pasta and peppers to the frying pan with the tomatoes and toss well. • Serve hot.

4 yellow bell peppers (capsicums)
$\frac{1}{3}$ cup (90 ml) extra-virgin olive oil
Salt
4 cloves garlic, finely chopped
1½ lb (750 g) tomatoes, peeled and chopped
1 tablespoon finely chopped fresh parsley
1 lb (500 g) maccheroni or other short pasta shape

SERVES 4–6

PREPARATION 10 min

COOKING 15 min

DIFFICULTY level 1

Fusilli

with pesto, cream, and tomatoes

Bring a large pot of salted water to a boil over high heat. • Mix the pesto and tomato sauce in a large bowl. Stir in the cream until well blended. • Cook the pasta in the boiling water until al dente. • Heat individual serving bowls with cooking water from the pasta. Discard the water. • Drain the pasta and transfer to the warmed bowls. Add the sauce, toss well, and serve hot.

½ cup (125 g) pesto (homemade – see page 20 – or storebought)

1 cup (250 ml) storebought unseasoned tomato sauce

⅓ cup (90 ml) heavy (double) cream

1 lb (500 g) fusilli

SERVES 4–6
PREPARATION 10 min
COOKING 15 min
DIFFICULTY level 1

Penne
with ricotta and pine nuts

Cook the pasta in a large pot of salted boiling water until al dente. • Toast the pine nuts in a large frying pan over medium heat until lightly browned, about 3 minutes. • Add the butter and let it melt. • Drain the pasta and add to the frying pan. Toss well for 1–2 minutes then remove from the heat. • Add the Parmesan and season with pepper. • Toss well and place in a serving dish. Arrange the ricotta on top. • Sprinkle with chives and serve hot.

1 lb (500 g) whole-wheat (wholemeal) or plain penne
1/4 cup (45 g) pine nuts
1/3 cup (90 g) butter
1/2 cup (60 g) freshly grated Parmesan
Freshly ground white pepper
5 oz (150 g) ricotta salata (or aged Pecorino) cheese, broken into bite size pieces
2 tablespoons finely chopped chives

SERVES 4–6

PREPARATION 10 min

COOKING 30 min

DIFFICULTY level 2

Penne

with asparagus and pine nuts

Bring a large pot of salted water to a boil over high heat. • Cook the asparagus in salted boiling water until tender, 5–8 minutes. • Drain well and then chop. • Toast the pine nuts in a large frying pan over medium heat until lightly browned, about 3 minutes. • Add the oil, garlic, and tomatoes. Season with salt and pepper. Sauté over low heat until the tomatoes begin to break down, about 15 minutes. • Beat the egg with 1 tablespoon of the Pecorino in a small bowl. Season with salt and pepper. • Meanwhile, cook the pasta in the boiling water until al dente. • Drain well and return to the pan. Add the egg mixture and over low heat until the egg cooks, about 2 minutes. • Transfer to a serving bowl. Add the tomato mixture and asparagus. Toss well. Sprinkle with Pecorino and serve hot.

1 lb (500 g) asparagus spears, tough stalks removed

1/4 cup (45 g) pine nuts

3 tablespoons extra-virgin olive oil

1 clove garlic, finely chopped

1 lb (500 g) ripe tomatoes, chopped

Salt and freshly ground black pepper

1 large egg

1/2 cup (60 g) freshly grated Pecorino or Parmesan

1 lb (500 g) whole-wheat (wholemeal) or plain penne

SERVES 4–6

PREPARATION 15 min

COOKING 2 h 10 min

DIFFICULTY level 2

Maccheroni
with spicy stewed brisket

Heat 2 tablespoons of the oil in a frying pan over medium heat. Add the brisket and sauté until lightly browned all over, 5–7 minutes. Remove from the heat. • Heat 2 tablespoons of the oil in a large saucepan over medium heat. Add the celery and onion, and sauté until the onion is softened, about 5 minutes. • Add the sautéed meat, the salami, endive, and water. Season with salt and pepper. Cover and simmer over low heat until the meat is very tender, about 2 hours. Remove from the heat. • Cook the pasta in a large pot of salted boiling water until al dente. • Drain well. Return the pasta to the pan. • Add the remaining oil, Parmesan, and parsley. Toss well. • Transfer the pasta to a serving dish. Spoon the stew onto the serving dish around the pasta. Season with pepper. • Serve hot.

½ cup (125 ml) extra-virgin olive oil
2 lb (1 kg) beef brisket,
    cut into bite-size chunks
2 celery sticks, chopped
1 large onion, chopped
5 oz (150 g) spicy salami,
    cut into small cubes
1 head broad leaf endive, chopped
Generous 2⅓ cups (600 ml) water,
    boiling
Salt and freshly ground black pepper
1 lb (500 g) maccheroni or other short
    pasta shape
¼ cup (30 g) freshly grated Parmesan
2 tablespoons finely chopped parsley

SERVES 4–6

PREPARATION 15 min

COOKING 35 min

DIFFICULTY level 1

Eliche
with spicy eggplant sauce

Bring a large pot of salted water to a boil over high heat. • Heat the oil in a large frying pan over medium heat. Add the garlic and sauté until pale golden brown, 2–3 minutes. • Add the eggplant and sauté until tender, about 10 minutes. • Season with salt and add the capers, parsley, and chile pepper. Mix well and cook for 2 minutes. • Meanwhile, cook the pasta in the boiling water until al dente. • Drain well and add to the eggplant mixture. Toss over high heat for 1 minute. Garnish with chopped eggs and serve at once.

⅓ cup (90 ml) extra-virgin olive oil
1 clove garlic, finely chopped
1 large eggplant (aubergine),
    cut into ¾ inch (2 cm) cubes
Salt
¼ cup (45 g) salt-cured capers,
    rinsed and chopped
2 tablespoons finely chopped parsley
1 red chile pepper, seeded and sliced
1 lb (500 g) eliche or other short
    pasta shape
2 hard-boiled eggs, shelled and chopped

42

SERVES 4–6

PREPARATION 15 min

COOKING 45 min

DIFFICULTY level 2

Baked Pasta
with eggplant

Cook the eggplant slices in batches on a hot grill pan or griddle until tender, about 5 minutes each batch. • Heat the stock in a large saucepan. Add the onion and simmer until tender, about 5 minutes. • Add the eggplant and season with salt and pepper. Remove from the heat. • Preheat the oven to 375°F (190°C/gas 5). • Cook the pasta in a large pot of salted boiling water until almost al dente. • Drain well and add to the eggplant mixture. • Transfer to an oiled baking dish. Sprinkle with the mozzarella. • Beat the milk and Parmesan in a bowl. Pour over the pasta. • Bake until lightly browned on top and the pasta is cooked through, about 15 minutes. • Serve hot.

2 lb (1 kg) eggplants (aubergines), thinly sliced
1/4 cup (60 ml) vegetable stock
1 large onion, thinly sliced
Salt and freshly ground black pepper
1 lb (500 g) maccheroni or other short pasta shape
6 oz (180 g) fresh mozzarella, drained and cut into 1/2 inch (1 cm) cubes
Generous 3/4 cup (200 ml) milk
1/2 cup (60 g) freshly grated Parmesan

SERVES 4–6

PREPARATION 10 min

COOKING 20 min

DIFFICULTY level 1

Penne
with scampi and chicory

Cook the pasta in a large pot of salted boiling water for 5 minutes. • Add the chicory and cook until the pasta is al dente. Drain well. • Meanwhile, heat the oil in a large frying pan over medium heat. Add the garlic and chile pepper and sauté until the garlic is pale golden brown, 2–3 minutes. • Add the scampi and sauté until tender, 3–5 minutes. • Add the pasta and chicory to the pan and mix well. Sauté for 2 minutes over high heat. Season with salt. • Serve hot.

1 lb (500 g) penne
2 lb (1 kg) chicory, coarsely chopped
1/4 cup (60 ml) extra-virgin olive oil
2 cloves garlic, finely chopped
1 red chile pepper, seeded and chopped
18 scampi, shelled and cut in half
Salt

SERVES 4–6

PREPARATION 15 min + 1 h to soak

COOKING 45 min

DIFFICULTY level 2

Penne

with mussels and tomatoes

Soak the mussels in a large bowl of cold water for 1 hour. Rinse well and scrub or pull of the beards. • Heat 2 tablespoons of the oil in a large saucepan. Add the garlic and sauté until pale golden brown, 2–3 minutes. • Add the mussels and cook over medium-high heat until they open, 7–10 minutes. Remove from the heat. Shell the mussels, discarding any that did not open. • Filter the cooking juices through a piece of muslin and set aside. • Heat the remaining oil in a large saucepan over medium heat. Add the pasta and mix well. Sauté for 2 minutes and then add the cooking juices from the mussels and the stock. • Cover and simmer over low heat for 5 minutes. • Add the potatoes and simmer for 5 minutes. Add the tomatoes and simmer until the pasta is al dente and the potatoes are tender, 5–10 minutes. Drain well and transfer to a heated serving bowl. • Add the mussels and basil, and season with salt and pepper. Toss well and sprinkle with the cheese. • Garnish with basil and serve hot.

2 lb (1 kg) fresh mussels, in shell
1/4 cup (60 ml) extra-virgin olive oil
2 cloves garlic, finely chopped
1 lb (500 g) penne
4 cups (1 liter) vegetable stock (homemade or bouillon cube), boiling, + extra, as required
1 lb (500 g) cherry tomatoes, halved
1 lb (500 g) potatoes, peeled and cut into 1/2 inch (1 cm) cubes
Leaves from 1 sprig of basil, torn + extra, to garnish
Salt and freshly ground black pepper
1/2 cup (60 g) freshly grated Pecorino or Parmesan

SERVES 4–6

PREPARATION 15 min + 30 min to chill

COOKING 15 min

DIFFICULTY level 1

Cool Fusilli

with tomatoes and onion

Cook the pasta in a large pot of salted boiling water until al dente. • Drain and cool under cold running water. Drain thoroughly and transfer to a large salad bowl. • Add 2 tablespoons of the oil and toss well. • Add the tomatoes, onion, garlic, basil, chile peppers, if using, and the remaining oil. Season with salt and toss well. • Serve at room temperature or chill in the refrigerator for 30 minutes.

1 lb (500 g) fusilli

⅓ cup (90 ml) extra-virgin olive oil

1½ lb (750 g) firm ripe salad tomatoes, peeled and coarsely chopped

1 sweet red Spanish onion, finely chopped

3 tablespoons finely chopped basil

2 cloves garlic, finely chopped

1–2 dried chile peppers, crumbled (optional)

Salt

SERVES 4–6

PREPARATION 15 min

COOKING 20 min

DIFFICULTY level 1

Spicy Fusilli
with swiss chard and pine nuts

Bring a large pot of salted water to a boil over high heat. • Cook the Swiss chard in a large saucepan of lightly salted water over medium heat until tender, 3–5 minutes. • Drain well and place in a bowl of cold water. Drain again, squeezing to remove excess moisture. • Melt the butter in a large frying pan over medium heat. Add the garlic and sauté until pale golden brown, 2–3 minutes. • Add the pine nuts and bread crumbs and sauté until golden brown and crisp, about 5 minutes. • Add the Swiss chard and the golden raisins. Mix well and sauté for 2 minutes. Season with salt. • Meanwhile, cook the pasta in the boiling water until al dente. • Drain well and add to the pan with the Swiss chard mixture. Add the chile pepper and toss over high heat for 2 minutes. • Serve hot.

1½ lb (750 g) Swiss chard (silver beet), shredded

Salt

⅓ cup (60 g) pine nuts

¼ cup (60 g) butter

2 cloves garlic, finely sliced

Scant 1½ cups (80 g) fresh bread crumbs

Scant ¼ cup (30 g) golden raisins (sultanas)

1 lb (500 g) whole-wheat (wholemeal) or plain fusilli

1 small red chile pepper, seeded and sliced

SERVES 4–6

PREPARATION 10 min

COOKING 20 min

DIFFICULTY level 1

Spirals
with chicory and watercress

Bring a large pot of salted water to a boil over high heat. • Melt the butter in a large saucepan over medium heat. Add the ham, mustard seeds, and apple. Season with salt and mix well. Sauté until the apple begins to soften and the ham is lightly browned, about 5 minutes. • Add the chicory and watercress and sauté until tender, 3–4 minutes. • Meanwhile, cook the pasta in the boiling water until al dente. • Drain well and add to the pan with the vegetable mixture. Season with pepper and toss over high heat for 2 minutes. • Serve hot.

3 tablespoons butter
5 oz (150 g) ham, chopped
1 teaspoon mustard seeds
1 red apple, cored and thinly sliced
Salt
4 small heads of chicory, chopped
12 oz (350 g) watercress
1 lb (500 g) spirals or other short pasta shape
Freshly ground black pepper

SERVES 4–6

PREPARATION 15 min

COOKING 30 min

DIFFICULTY level 1

Farfalle

with beans and zucchini

Bring a large pot of salted water to a boil over high heat. • Heat the oil in a large frying pan over medium heat. Add the onions and garlic and sauté until softened, about 5 minutes. • Add the water, zucchini, arugula, and bay leaf. Sauté for 2 minutes. • Add the wine and cook until it evaporates, 2–3 minutes. • Simmer until the zucchini are tender, about 5 minutes. • Add the beans and simmer for 5 more minutes, adding more water if the mixture sticks to the pan. Discard the bay leaf. Season with salt and pepper. • Meanwhile, cook the pasta in the boiling water until al dente. • Drain, reserving 5 tablespoons of the cooking liquid. • Add the pasta and cooking liquid to the pan. Toss over high heat for 1 minute. Add the parsley and season with pepper. • Sprinkle with cheese and serve hot.

2 tablespoons extra-virgin olive oil
2 spring onions, sliced
1 clove garlic, finely chopped
1 tablespoon water
4 large zucchini (courgettes), thinly sliced
3 oz (90 g) arugula (rocket), chopped
1 bay leaf
1/2 cup (125 ml) dry white wine
1 (14-oz/ 400-g) can borlotti or red kidney beans, drained
Salt and freshly ground black pepper
1 lb (500 g) farfalle
2 tablespoons finely chopped parsley
1 oz (30 g) Parmesan, cut into flakes

Farfalle
with sautéed vegetables

Bring a large pot of salted water to a boil over high heat. • Heat 1 tablespoon of oil in a large frying pan over medium heat. Add the pine nuts and sauté until lightly browned, 2–3 minutes. Set aside. • Add the remaining oil to the frying pan. Add the shallots and garlic and sauté until softened, about 5 minutes. • Add the zucchini, mushrooms, bell pepper, and carrots. Sauté over medium heat until the vegetables are softened, 5–7 minutes. • Sprinkle with thyme and season with salt and pepper. • Meanwhile, cook the pasta in the boiling water until al dente. • Drain well and add to the pan with the vegetables. Toss over high heat for 1 minute. Sprinkle with the pine nuts and Parmesan and serve hot.

1/4 cup (60 ml) extra-virgin olive oil
1/4 cup (45 g) pine nuts
2 shallots, finely chopped
2 cloves garlic, finely chopped
6 small zucchini (courgettes), sliced
12 oz (350 g) button mushrooms, sliced
1 large yellow bell pepper (capsicum), seeded and sliced
3 large carrots, cut into julienne strips
2 tablespoons finely chopped thyme
Salt and freshly ground black pepper
1 lb (500 g) farfalle
1/2 cup (60 g) freshly grated Parmesan

SERVES 4–6

PREPARATION 10 min

COOKING 20 min

DIFFICULTY level 1

Penne
with zucchini, ham, and pistachios

Bring a large pot of salted water to a boil over high heat. • Heat the oil in a large frying pan over medium heat. Add the white part of the scallions. Sauté until they begin to soften, 2 minutes. • Add the wine and let evaporate for 3 minutes. • Add the zucchini and season with salt. Mix well and sauté until the zucchini are tender, about 5 minutes. • Add the ham, pistachios, and half the green part of the scallions. Mix well and cook for 1 minute. Season with pepper. • Meanwhile, cook the pasta in the boiling water until al dente. • Drain well and add to the pan with the zucchini. Toss over high heat for 1 minute. • Add the butter and Parmesan and toss well. • Sprinkle with the remaining scallions and serve hot.

1/4 cup (60 ml) extra-virgin olive oil
8 scallions (spring onions), white and green parts sliced separately
1/3 cup (90 ml) dry white wine
8 small zucchini (courgettes), cut into small cubes
Salt
8 oz (250 g) smoked ham, cut into small cubes
2/3 cup (100 g) blanched pistachios, coarsely chopped
Freshly ground black pepper
1 lb (500 g) penne
3 tablespoons butter
1/2 cup (60 g) freshly grated Parmesan

Fusilli

with capers and anchovies

Bring a large pot of salted water to a boil over high heat. • Heat 4 tablespoons of the oil in a small frying pan over medium-low heat. Add the anchovies and stir until they have dissolved into the oil, about 5 minutes. Remove from the heat and set aside. • Heat the remaining oil in a large frying pan over medium heat. Add the garlic and sauté until softened, 2–3 minutes. • Cook the pasta in the boiling water until al dente. • Drain well and add to the pan with the garlic and oil. Add the anchovy mixture and toss gently over medium heat for 1 minute. • Serve hot.

⅔ cup (150 ml) extra-virgin olive oil

4 salt cured anchovies or 8 anchovy fillets, rinsed and chopped

4 cloves garlic, finely chopped

4 tablespoons salt-cured capers, rinsed

1–2 teaspoons hot paprika

1 lb (500 g) fusilli

Fusilli

with spinach, onions, and capers

Bring a large pot of salted water to a boil over high heat. • Heat 2 tablespoons of oil in a large frying pan over medium heat. Add the onions, capers, and anchovies and sauté for 5 minutes. Add 2 tablespoons of hot water and simmer low heat for 10 minutes. • Blanch the spinach in a little salted, boiling water for 3–4 minutes. Drain well. • Meanwhile, cook the pasta in the boiling water. • Heat the remaining oil in a large frying pan and sauté the garlic until pale golden brown, 3–4 minutes. Add the spinach to the oil. • Drain the pasta, and add to the pan with the spinach. Toss gently for 1 minute. • Top with the onion sauce and olives and serve hot.

½ cup (125 ml) extra-virgin olive oil
2 medium onions, thinly sliced
8–10 salt-cured anchovy fillets
2 tablespoons salt-cured capers, rinsed
1 lb (500 g) fusilli
2 lb (1 kg) spinach, chopped
2 cloves garlic, finely chopped
⅔ cup (60 g) black olives

SERVES 4–6

PREPARATION 45 min

COOKING 30 min

DIFFICULTY level 2

Maccheroni
with meatballs

Place the milk in a small bowl and add the bread. • Place the beef, prosciutto, parsley, and garlic in a food processor and chop until smooth. • Transfer to a bowl and add the well-squeezed bread, egg yolk, lemon zest, and nutmeg. Season with salt and pepper and mix well. • Shape the mixture into balls about the size of a marble and roll in the flour. Set aside. • Bring a large pot of salted water to a boil over high heat. • Heat the oil in a large frying pan and sauté the onion until translucent. • Add the tomatoes and oregano and cook over medium heat for 10–15 minutes. Season with salt and pepper. • Cook the meatballs in a medium pan of simmering water for 3 minutes. Scoop out with a slotted spoon and drain on a clean cloth. • Cook the pasta in the boiling water until al dente. • Drain and add to the pan with the tomato sauce. • Add the meatballs and toss gently over medium heat for 1–2 minutes. • Sprinkle with the Parmesan and serve hot.

$^1/_3$ cup (90 ml) milk
2 thick slices of day-old bread, crusts removed, crumbled
1 lb (500 g) ground (minced) beef
4 oz (125 g) prosciutto (Parma ham)
Small bunch parsley
1 clove garlic
1 egg yolk
Finely grated zest of 1 lemon
Pinch of nutmeg
Salt and freshly ground black pepper
$^1/_2$ cup (75 g) all-purpose (plain) flour
5 tablespoons extra-virgin olive oil
1 small onion, finely chopped
2 lb (1 kg) tomatoes, peeled and chopped
1 teaspoon dried oregano
1 lb (500 g) maccheroni
$^1/_2$ cup (60 g) freshly grated Parmesan

Baked Rigatoni
with ham and mushrooms

Bring a large pot of salted water to a boil over high heat. • Preheat the oven to 400°F (200°C/gas 6). • Butter a large baking dish. • Mix half the Parmesan into the Béchamel. • Sauté the mushrooms in 2 tablespoons of the butter in a frying pan over high heat until pale gold, 2–3 minutes. • Add the ham and sauté until crisp, about 5 minutes. • Meanwhile, cook the pasta in the boiling water until just al dente. • Drain and place half in the baking dish. Top with half the mushrooms and ham. Cover with half the Béchamel. Make a second layer with the pasta, mushrooms, ham, and Béchamel. Sprinkle with the remaining Parmesan and dot with the remaining butter. • Bake until the surface is golden brown, 10–15 minutes. • Serve hot.

½ cup (60 g) freshly grated Parmesan

2 cups (500 ml) Béchamel sauce (made with 3 tablespoons butter, 3 tablespoons flour, and 2 cups/ 500 ml milk)

5 oz (150 g) white mushrooms, thinly sliced

¼ cup (60 g) butter, cut into flakes

¾ cup (90 g) diced ham

1 lb (500 g) dried pasta tubes, such as rigatoni

5 oz (150 g) prosciutto (Parma ham), cut into thin strips

Baked Fusilli,
with tomatoes and cheese

Heat 3 tablespoons of oil and 1 tablespoon of butter in a medium saucepan over low heat. Add the onion and garlic and sauté until softened, about 5 minutes. • Add the prosciutto, parsley, basil, and tomatoes and season with salt and pepper. Simmer until the tomatoes have broken down, 15–20 minutes. • Purée the mixture in a blender and set aside. • Cook the pasta in a large pot of salted boiling water until al dente. Drain well. • Melt the remaining butter over the pasta and drizzle with the remaining oil. Season with pepper. • Preheat the oven to 400°F (200°C/gas 6). • Spoon half the pasta into an oiled baking dish, top with half the meat sauce, and sprinkle with half the Pecorino. • Cover with the remaining pasta, meat sauce, and Pecorino. • Bake until the golden brown, 10–15 minutes. • Let stand for 15 minutes before serving.

⅓ cup (90 ml) extra-virgin olive oil
¼ cup (60 g) butter
1 clove garlic, lightly crushed but whole
½ red onion, finely sliced
4 oz (125 g) prosciutto (Parma ham), finely chopped
Leaves from 1 bunch fresh parsley, finely chopped
Leaves from 1 bunch fresh basil, finely chopped
6 tomatoes, peeled and seeded
Salt and freshly ground black pepper
12 oz (350 g) fusilli or other short pasta shape
½ cup (60 g) freshly grated Pecorino

Index

Copyright © 2007 by McRae Books Srl

This English edition first published in 2007

All rights reserved. No part of this book may be reproduced in any form without the prior written permission of the publisher and copyright owner.

Penne, Fusilli & Co.

was created and produced by McRae Books Srl

Borgo Santa Croce, 8 – Florence (Italy)

info@mcraebooks.com

Publishers: Anne McRae and Marco Nardi

Project Director: Anne McRae

Design: Sara Mathews

Text: Carla Bardi

Editing: Osla Fraser

Photography: Cristina Canepari, Keeho Casati, Gil Gallo, Walter Mericchi, Sandra Preussinger

Home Economist: Benedetto Rillo

Artbuying: McRae Books

Layouts: Adina Stefania Dragomir

Repro: Fotolito Raf, Florence

ISBN 978-88-89272-81-7

Printed and bound in China